# ROYAL GORGE
## Photography by Eve Nagode

Published by Fox Run Art Press
306 Main St., Ste 546
Cañon City, Colorado 81212
FoxRunArt.com

© 2015, 2017 Fox Run Art Press
© 2015, 2017 Eve Nagode
All rights reserved. First, second & third editions 2015
Fourth edition 2017

Printed in Korea
25 24 23 22 21 20 19 18 17    4 5 6 7
ISBN: 978-0-9962792-3-9
Library of Congress Control Number: 2015906027

No portion of this book may be
reproduced without written permission
from the publisher.

Front Cover: Award winning photo of sunrise on the Royal Gorge Bridge
Back Cover: View from Point Sublime
Title Page: Sunrise behind Fremont Peak
Facing Page: Sunset through the branches of a burned tree
Overleaf: Burned trees and scorched earth on the south side of the Park
Final Page: Moonrise over Fremont Peak

# June 11, 2013

Ask any local resident about that day and chances are they will pick up their cell phone or tablet and show you a picture of the first sign of trouble. There, against a clear cerulean sky, rises a towering column of smoke directly behind Fremont Peak. The wildfire, which took five days to contain, burned 3,218 acres of juniper and pine forest. The Royal Gorge Bridge & Park, a popular Colorado tourist attraction, lost 48 of 52 structures. The famous bridge stood majestically over the rubble with only 100 of its over 1,200 wooden planks charred from the fire.

Cleanup began as soon as the Park was safe to enter. Plans were made to replace attractions built over eighty-four years. Black-water runoff into the Arkansas River was a threat to the Cañon City Water Treatment Plant directly downstream. Funds were obtained to hydro-ax and replant the burn scar to stabilize the exposed surface of the soil.

The photographs in this book start in the summer of 2013 and continue into the spring of 2015. Many of the images capture the park when it was closed to the public during reconstruction. Some of the rare night sky images were taken in 2014 when the park had no electricity.

I hope you enjoy this visual journey during the restoration of the Royal Gorge. I especially wish to thank the Royal Gorge Bridge & Park for allowing me extraordinary access to the Park during its reconstruction. This book is dedicated to my husband, Bob, for his never-ending enthusiastic support for this project.

*Enjoy the journey!*

Eve Nagode
FoxRunArt.com
Cañon City, Colorado

Heat from the fire broke the cable and melted the aluminum siding on the tram which had been in operation since 1969.

The fire burned off the colorful coatings on the carousel animals leaving the fiberglass bodies so brittle they fell apart when moved.

For 20 years visitors of all ages enjoyed riding the carousel.

To help stabilize water run-off from the burn scar, wildflower and grass seeds were spread via helicopter during the first winter after the fire.

Preceding pages: Dead trees line the south rim of the gorge. The building on the right is next to where the south tram terminal was located.

Standing over the smoke-stained rocks, a forest of dead trees await mulching by the hydro-ax equipment.

This cluster of trees was saved from hydro-axing so wildlife could nest in the cavities.

Just two months after the fire, native wildflowers, scrub oak and grasses flourish in the midst of the burn scar.

A year after the fire, wildflowers bloom amongst the chunks of wood left by hydro-axing.

One year after the fire, green grasses and wildflowers return to the burn scar as viewed from Point Sublime. During the hydro-axing process, clusters of dead trees were left standing to break up the landscape and provide some shelter for the wildlife.

Hope returns to the Royal Gorge Park as the Visitor Center rebuild begins. The light green fields on the left show new growth on the burn scar after aerial seeding and hydro-axing the dead trees.

Rocky Mountain bighorns have balance-aiding split hooves and rough hoof bottoms for a natural grip to help them move easily on the rocks.

Mature males spend most of their year in bachelor flocks apart from groups of females and young sheep.

During the mating season or "rut," the rams join the female groups and engage in fierce competition to establish access rights to ewes.

Bighorn sheep protect themselves from predators by facing different directions, allowing them to keep watch on their surroundings.

The Rocky Mountain bighorn sheep was designated the official state animal of Colorado in 1961.

A turkey vulture sits on the railing near the north tower of the bridge.

Mule deer are common in the Park, but don't feed them. It's against the law in Colorado to feed any big-game animal.

As the ecosystem recovers, young deer play and thrive under the burned trees.

Affectionately called the "Royal Gorge Eagles," turkey vultures are frequently seen in the Park during the summer.

The reflected color of the Royal Gorge granite changes depending on the time of day and year. A mid-summer sunset shines behind a small tree growing out of a rock near the north tower of the bridge.

The same tree is seen during a winter morning sunrise that glows on the Grand Canyon Hills in the distance.

Overleaf: The Royal Gorge Park consists of over 5,000 acres surrounding the Royal Gorge Bridge. This winter sunrise view of the eastern side of the Park shows Fremont Peak to the left and the Arkansas River winding its way towards Cañon City, Colorado.

The Arkansas River flows east through the Royal Gorge as seen from the north end of the bridge.

This frozen waterfall on the south side of the Park is only visible from the air.

A "powdered sugar" view of Fremont Peak is seen from the bridge after a heavy winter snowfall.

An early morning view of the burn scar from Point Sublime shows the trees that will be hydro-axed into mulch.

This view of the Royal Gorge Bridge will be partially blocked on the right when the new Visitor Center and gondola tower are completed. A new restaurant and entertainment stage will be built on the empty plaza on the left.

Snow evaporation creates an early morning haze in an aerial view of the bridge looking east across the cliffs of the Royal Gorge.

The Royal Gorge was originally named the Grand Canyon of the Arkansas. Confusion with the *other* Grand Canyon led to renaming it the Royal Gorge. In this view looking west, the Arkansas River enters the beginning of the gorge. In the distance the sunrise shines on the Grand Canyon Hills which retain the original name.

This unique view of the south side of the Park before re-construction shows an open Park without buildings and fences. The ancient juniper in the foreground miraculously escaped the destruction around it.

Engine #499 survived with some heat damage and loss of the wooden doghouse on the tender.
Behind the engine, sat the red D&RGW Caboose #0584 which was destroyed in the fire.

Sunrise shines on the hills behind the south tower of the bridge.

The north tower of the bridge rises over the Royal Gorge as seen from the Royal Gorge Route Railroad.

A rare view of the underside of the bridge shows the original 1929 construction.

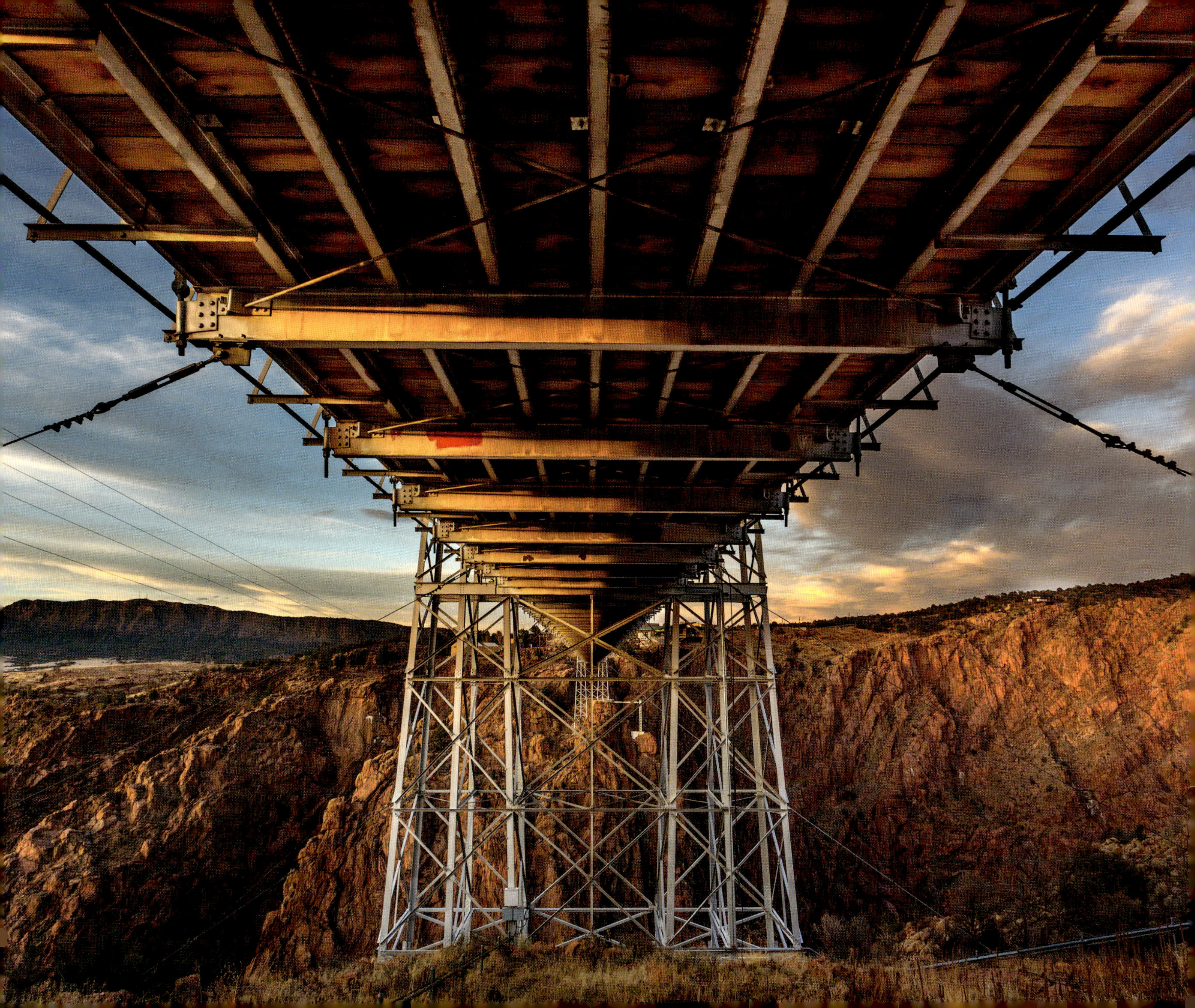

A sunrise view shows two buildings that survived the fire. The look-out building on the left was constructed in 1952 and is the oldest remaining wooden structure in the Park.

Looking east at the Royal Gorge from the north tower of the bridge, you can see the new Visitor Center on the left and Point Sublime through the tower.

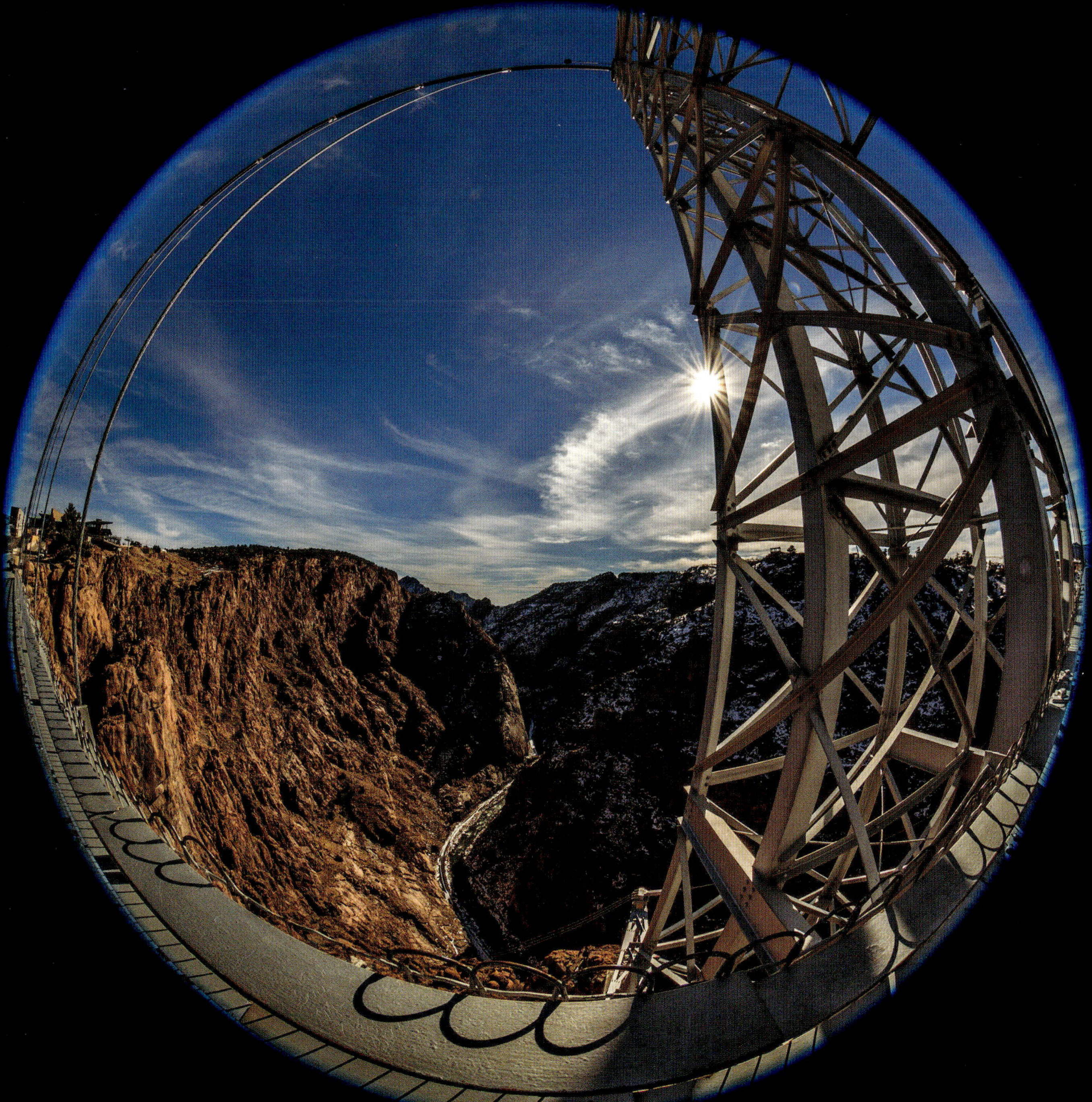

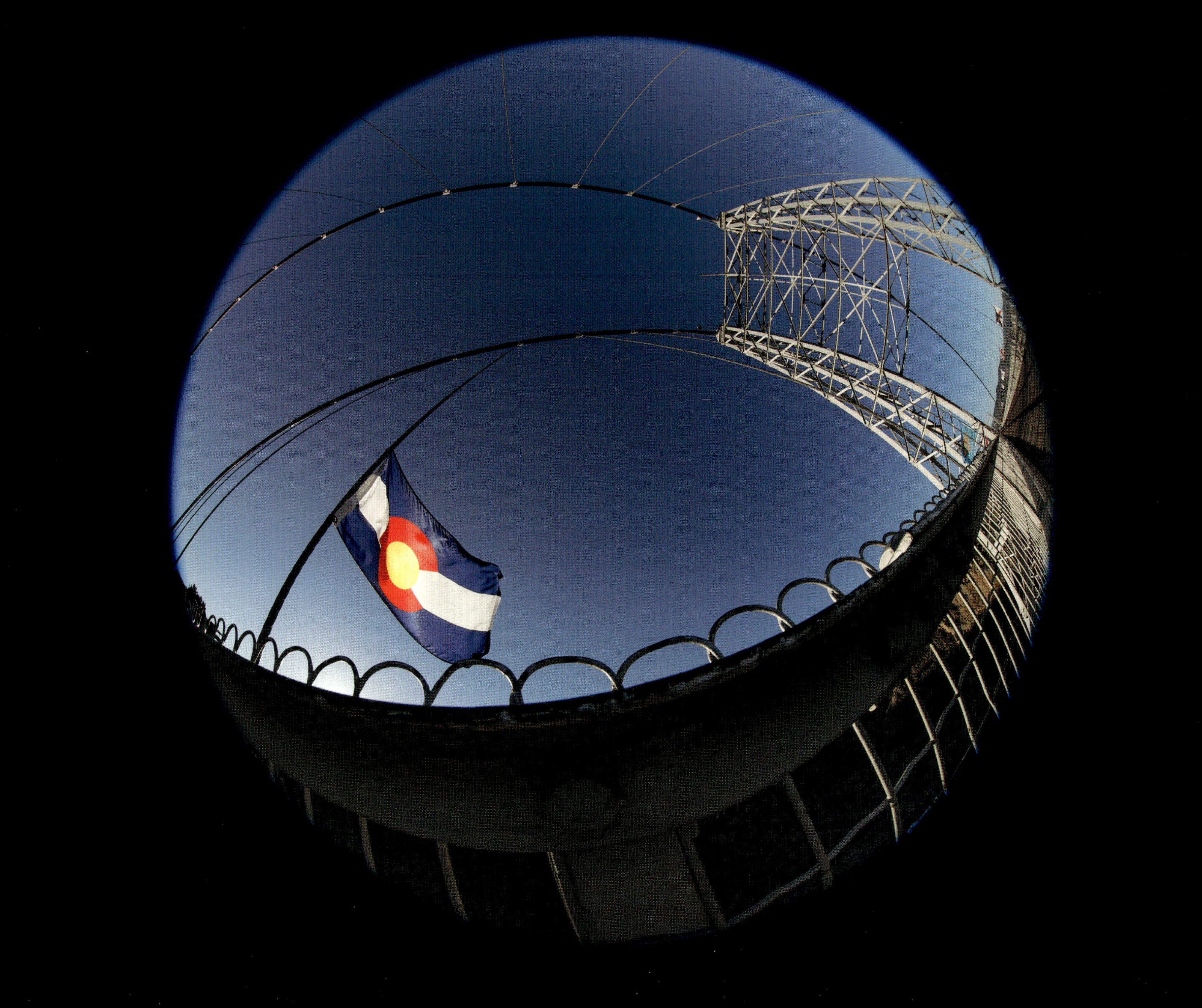

Looking up at the bridge tower you can see four of the state flags.

During the summer, flags from each state are displayed on the bridge. This one belongs to Colorado.

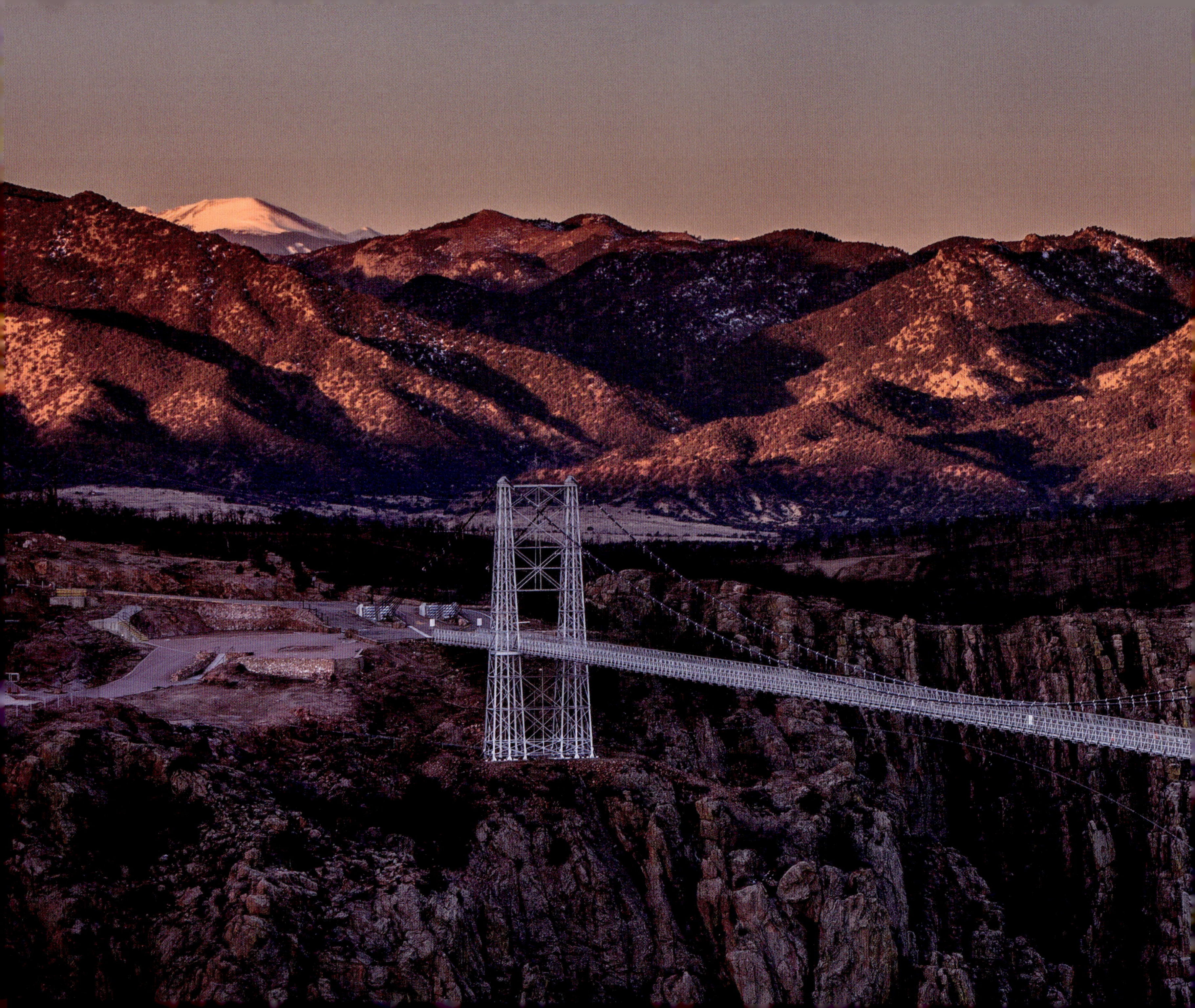

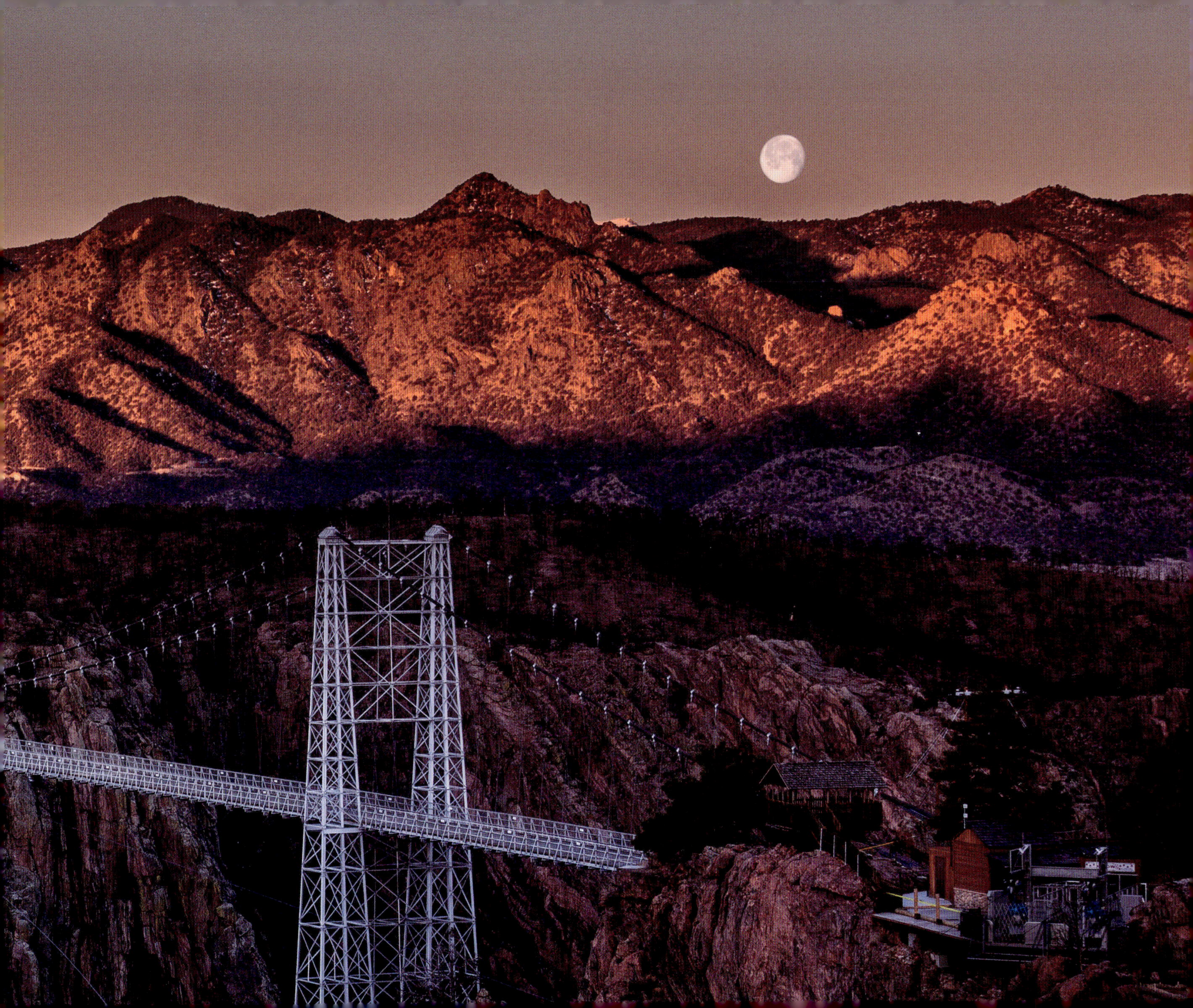

In this photo of the eclipse of the moon on October 8, 2014, you can see details of the original bridge construction.

Previous page: The full moon at sunrise shines over the bridge. Burned trees stretch across the south rim.

Another eclipse of the moon shines over the Sangres de Cristo mountains at sunrise. Photo was taken from the north side of the Park on April 4, 2015.

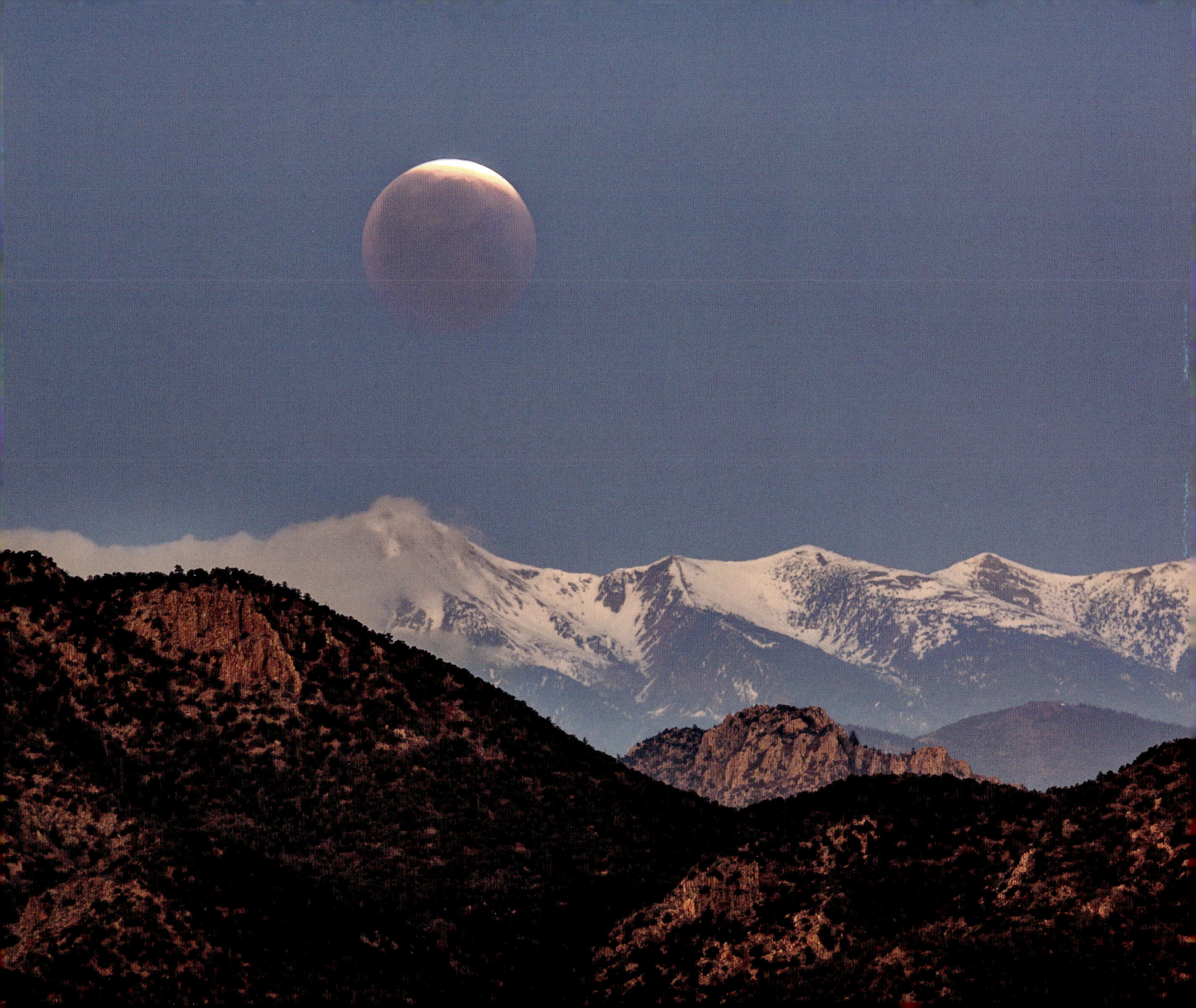

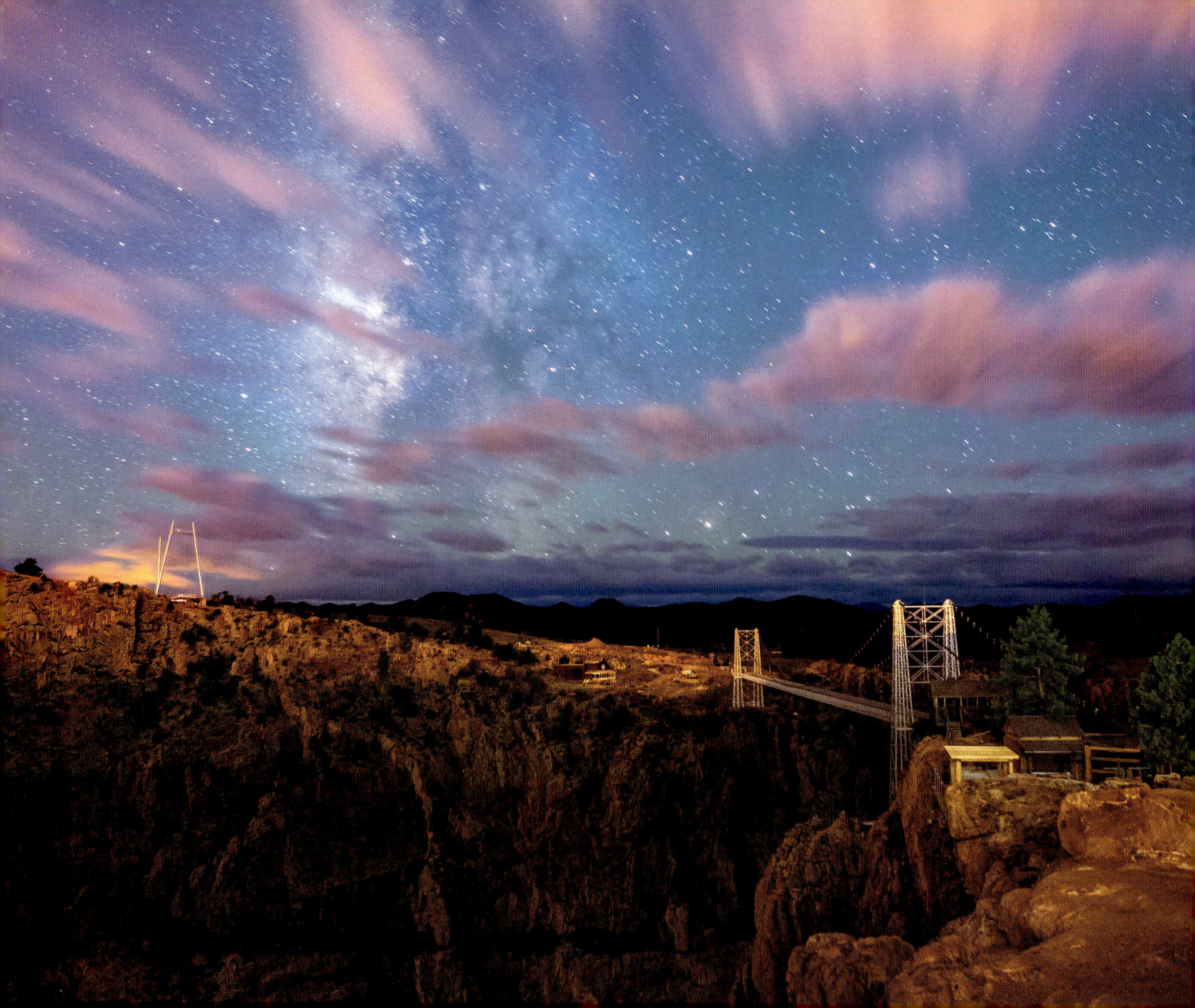

Stars shine over the bridge during the summer of 2014.

Steam engine 499 was built in 1902 as a standard gauge, and rebuilt in 1930 as a class K-37 narrow gauge.

The Royal Gorge train stops at the hanging railroad bridge which was built in 1879. Next to the bridge is the platform at the base of the Incline Railway.

Completed in 1931, the Incline Railway was one of the world's steepest funiculars traveling into the gorge diagonally 1500 feet at a 45 degree angle. The incline control system was damaged beyond repair in the fire. The cars sustained minor damage.

Gaps between some of the planks on the bridge are wide enough to see the Arkansas River and railroad tracks below. Next to the river you can also see the original wooden water pipeline that was used to supply water to Cañon City.

In the winter, snow can get so deep on the bridge that you cannot see the planks at all.

Sunset shines on the cliffs as seen from the south tower.

A rainstorm soaks the wooden planks on the bridge under the south tower. The new cable anchors installed in the 1980s look like a pair of giant shoes.

This sunrise view was taken during reconstruction. The burned forest can be seen in the background.

In the 1980s, new cable wires replaced the lower cables. In this photo you can see the joints between the original wires coming down from the top of the tower (reddish brown) and the new wires (gray).

Wind cables, added in the 1980's to reduce the sway of the bridge, frame the steelwork for the new Visitor Center.

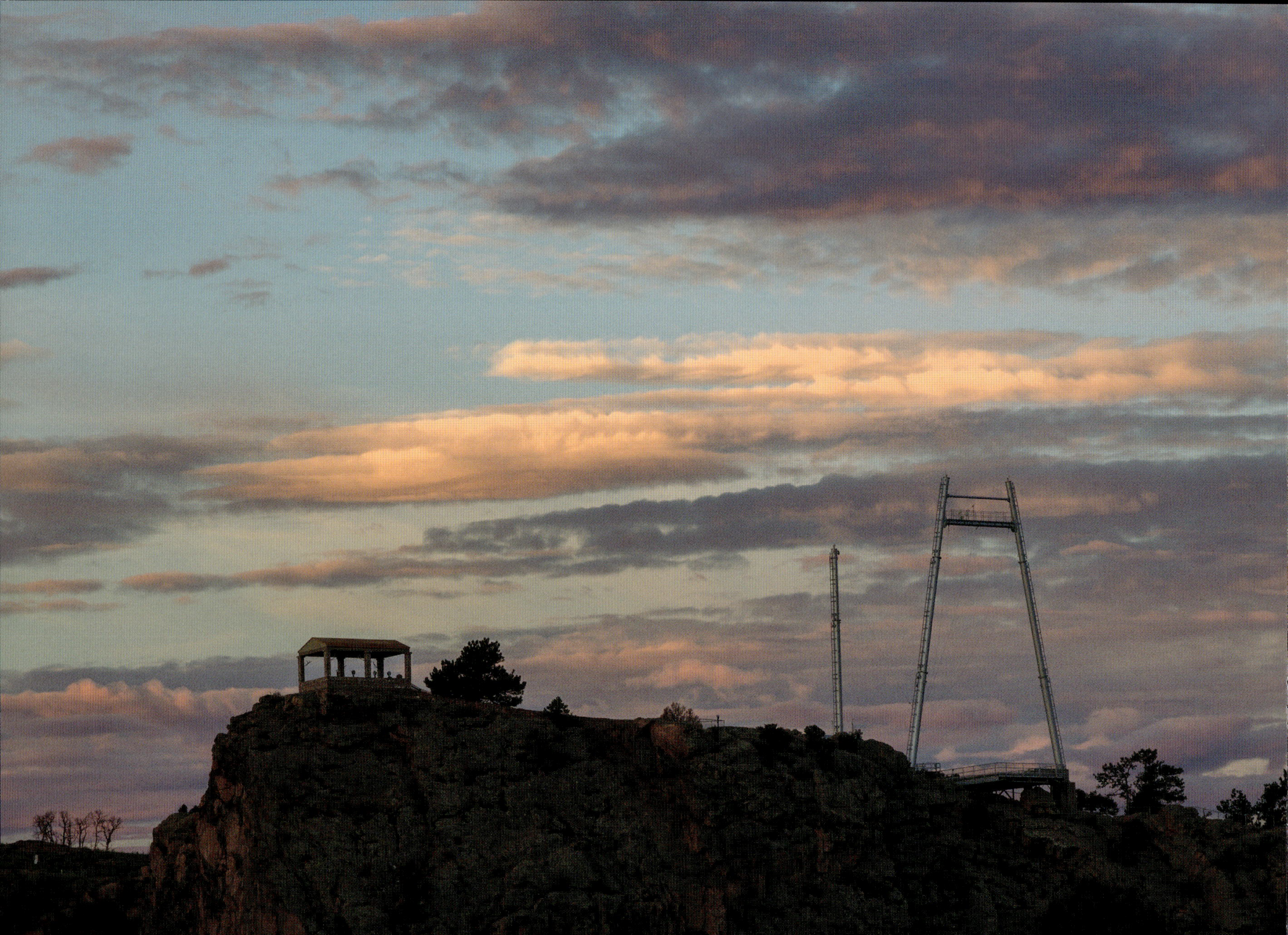

The graceful beauty of the bridge is shown in these silhouettes from on the bridge, below the bridge and in the air.

The original roof on the building at Point Sublime burned in the Royal Gorge Fire and was replaced. The Skycoaster ride was not damaged by the fire.

# Ready to Rebuild the New Visitor Center
## January 30, 2014

The Plaza Theater was the only structure near the south tower of the bridge to survive the fire. Firefighters removed the burning wood steps before the intense smoke and heat of the fire forced them to leave.

On the ridge behind the Plaza Theater stood Mountain Man Camp which was completely destroyed.

Smoke from the fire was first seen rising from behind the hills on the south side of the bridge.

Two small buildings close to the north tower of the bridge were all that remained of the Visitor Center complex.

Smoke stains were cleaned from the quartz stone walls of the Incline building. The damaged building, built in 1931, was later removed.

## Partial List of Park Features Damaged or Destroyed

Visitors Center (Tram North Station)
Eagles Nest Gift Shop (Tram South Station)
Aerial Tram
Incline Railway
Stryker Rich Trading Post
Main Gate
Carousel
Trolley
Water Clock
Royal Village Shirt Shop
Entertainment Gazebo

Royal Smokehouse & BBQ
Point Sublime Roof
Bridge Crew Creamery
Magic Shack
Juniper Junction
Children's Playground
Soaring Eagle Zipline
Inspiration Point
Water Treatment Plant
Dog Kennels
All Public Restrooms

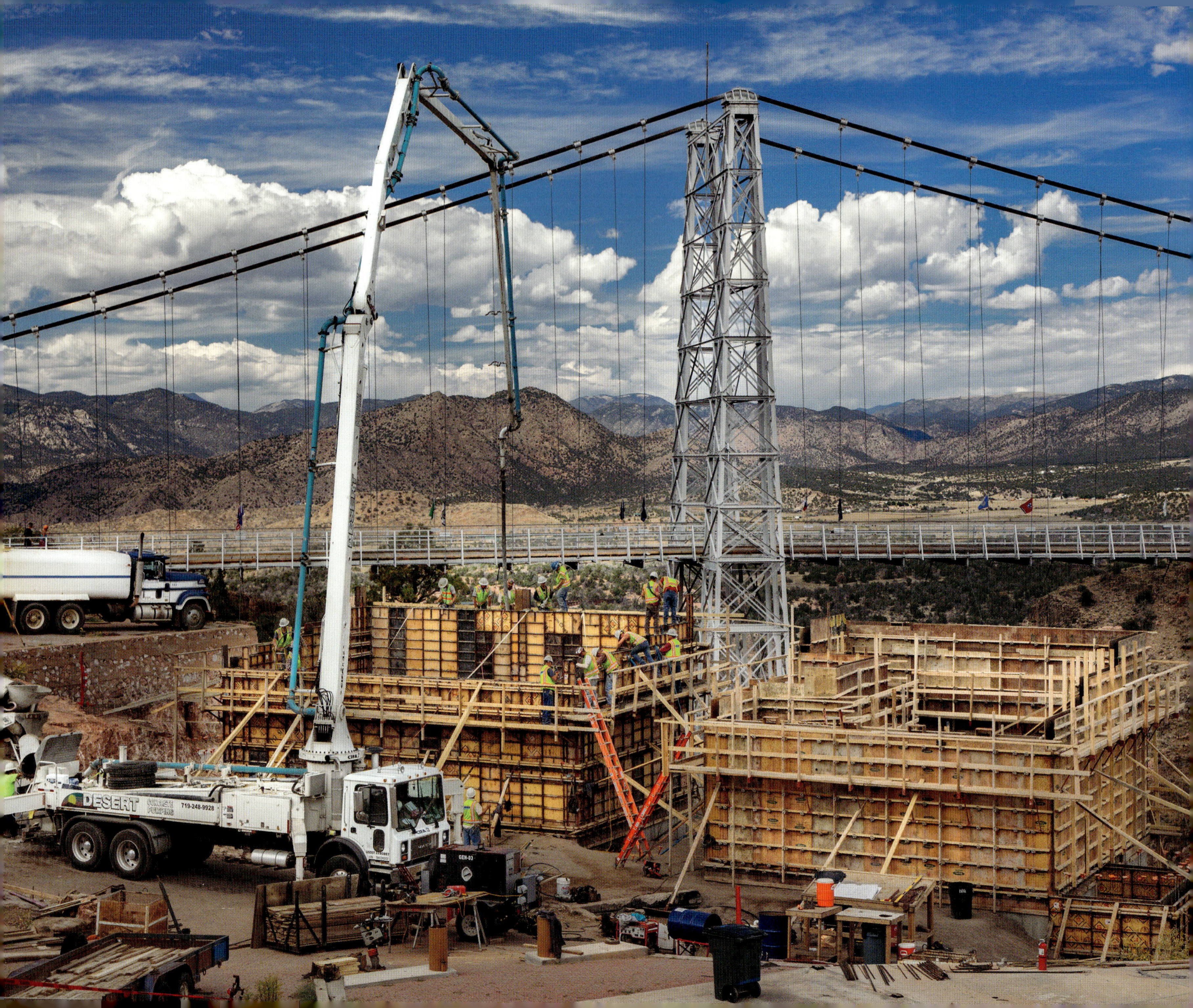
DESERT
719-248-9928

The concrete pour for the Visitor Center was completed at dawn to allow time for the foundation to setup in the cold winter weather.

Ironworkers installed the complex steel frame of the Visitor Center.

Roofers placed fire-resistant metal panels on the Visitor Center. In the background is the profile of the John F. Kennedy Mountain.

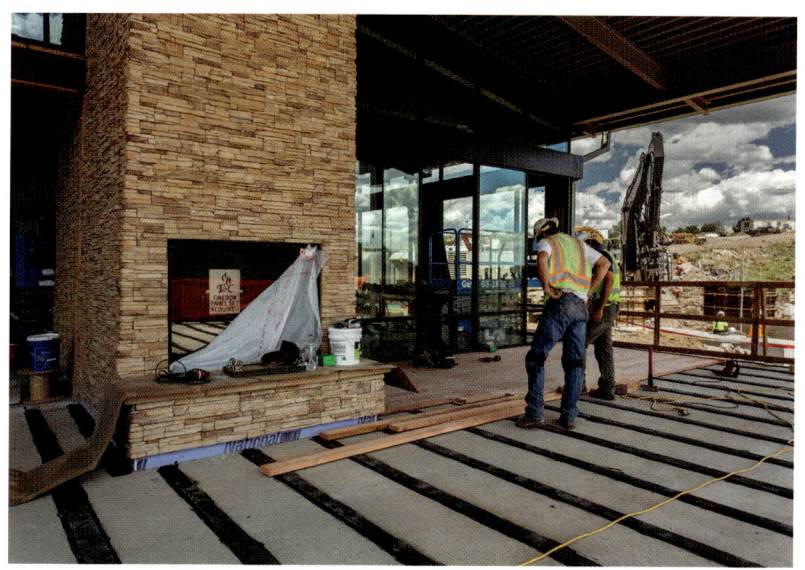

Carpenters laid out the boards on the new Visitor Center deck.

Solid concrete was poured into the walls of the new restaurant and public restroom next to the south tower.

The new gondolas replaced the old aerial tram and glide 2,400 feet across the Royal Gorge.

The Plaza Theater got a face lift and features park videos and live entertainment.

Overleaf: Back in business again! Aerial view of the new gondolas crossing the Royal Gorge.

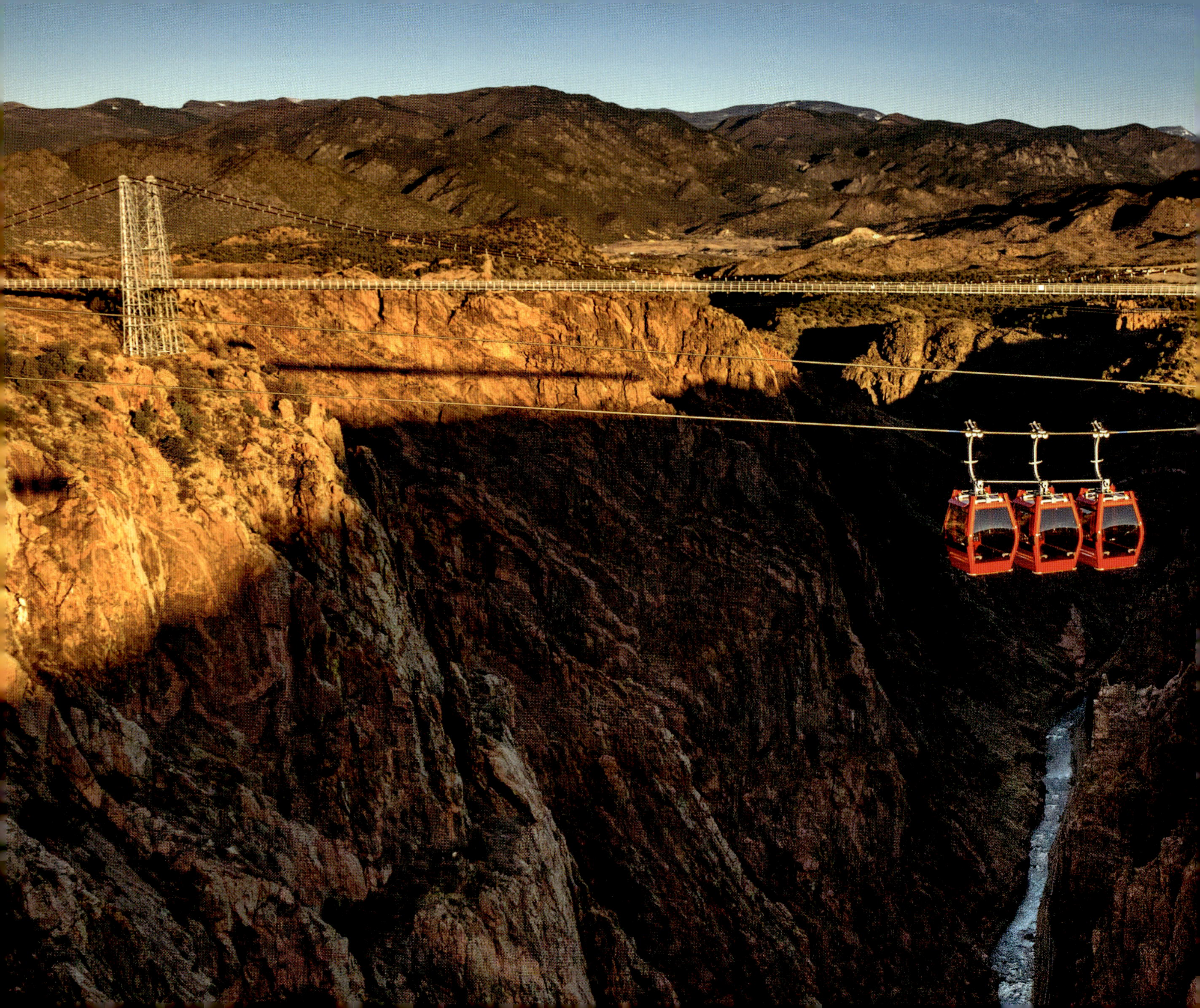

## Artist Statement

I like to tell stories, sometimes in a single image and sometimes as a series. I treat my subjects like digital paintings inspired by real-life events. Careful thought is put into composition and light. If my photographs speak to the viewer on an emotional level or bring back a personal memory, then I have succeeded in my work.

## About the Artist

My father passed on to me his love for taking pictures. That is why I chose photography as my major at Rhode Island School of Design. After I received my BFA, I worked as a photographer and graphic designer. Eventually, this led to a corporate career where my daily life had little to do with the fine arts. I think I was waiting for the creative freedom of digital technology.

I retired in 2010 and moved to Cañon City, Colorado where I became active in photography, entering shows and winning awards. When the Royal Gorge Bridge & Park burned down in June 2013, I asked RGB&P management if I could document the rebuild and restoration. The bridge and scenic gorge became my mentor in the beauty of the changing light throughout the day. For more examples of my work, please visit my website: FoxRunArt.com

*Eve Nagode, Fox Run Art*